Seeds of a Nation

California

P. M. Boekhoff and Stuart A. Kallen

KidHaven Press, an imprint of Gale Group, Inc.

P.O. Box 289009, San Diego, CA 92198-9009

L. E. SMOOT MEMORIAL LIBRARY
9533 KINGS HIGHWAY
KING GEORGE, VA 22485

Picture Credits

On Cover: *Father Serra Celebrates Mass at Monterey*
Cover Photo: California Historical Society
© Art Resource, NY, 36
© Bettmann/CORBIS, 12
© Christie's Images/CORBIS, 9 (bottom)
© Philip James Corwin/CORBIS, 26
© Richard Cummins/CORBIS, 17
© Ecoscene/CORBIS, 10
© Michael Freeman/CORBIS, 18
© Robert Holmes/CORBIS, 7
© Lowell Georgia/CORBIS, 35
Hulton Getty Collection/Archive Photos, 24
Chris Jouan, 5, 21, 39
© Craig Lovell/CORBIS, 23
© David Muench/CORBIS, 14, 19
North Wind Picture Archive, 15, 22, 27, 31, 32, 42
© Stock Montage, Inc., 28, 29, 37, 41
© Robert Taylor/Art Resource, NY, 9 (top)

Library of Congress Cataloging-in-Publication Data

Boekhoff, P. M. (Patti Marlene), 1957–
   California / by P. M. Boekhoff and Stuart A. Kallen.
      p. cm. — (Seeds of a nation)
   Includes bibliographical references (p.).
   Summary: Discusses the earliest inhabitants and natural resources of
   California, the arrival of European explorers, the establishment of
   Spanish missions, the Mexican War, the gold rush, and statehood.
   ISBN 0-7377-0946-4 (alk. paper)
   1. California—History—To 1846—Juvenile literature. 2. California—
   History—1846–1850—Juvenile literature. [1. California—History—
   To 1846. 2. California—History—1846–1850.] I. Kallen, Stuart A.,
   1955– II. Title. III. Series.
   F864 .B63 2002
   979.4—dc21

   2001001862

   Copyright 2002 by KidHaven Press, an imprint of Gale Group, Inc.
      P.O. Box 289009, San Diego, CA, 92198-9009

No part of this book may be reproduced or used in any other form or by any
other means, electrical, mechanical, or otherwise, including, but not limited
to photocopying, recording, or any information storage and retrieval system,
without prior written permission from the publisher.

Printed in the U.S.A.

Contents

Chapter One

The First Californians

California is the most populated state in the country, and it is known for its natural beauty, productive farms, and movie and television industry. The state is bordered by Oregon to the north, Nevada and Arizona to the east, Mexico to the south, and the Pacific Ocean to the west.

The first Californians were Native Americans who lived in the area for more than ten thousand years. Scholars estimate that three hundred thousand to 1 million Native Americans lived in the state by the 1500s. These people spoke over 135 varieties of 60 different languages.

The tribes lived in more than five hundred small communities, each one averaging a few hundred people, with well-defined borders between different groups.

The villages were filled with houses made from wood, bark, reeds, or mud depending on the tribe. In the cool damp northern woods, Native Americans built large rectangular houses of cedar or redwood planks lashed to a post-and-beam framework. In wooded or mountainous areas, small, warm, watertight shelters were made out of redwood, cedar, or pine slabs leaned together in a tepee shape. Houses were heated by open fires built in pits dug in the center of each dwelling. Smoke from the fire was vented through a hole in the roof.

CALIFORNIA'S PLACE IN THE UNITED STATES TODAY

The Northern Tribes

California tribes such as the Tolowa, Yurok, Hupa, and Shasta lived mainly along the ocean and Klamath River in the northwest part of the state.

The Yurok were hunters who caught fish with harpoons while standing in boats carved from redwood trees. Their Hupa neighbors often traded seeds, nuts, and deerskins for Yurok boats and dried fish.

In northeast California, tribes such as the Modoc and Achumawi lived in the high barren Modoc Plateau and the Cascade Mountains east of present-day Weed, California. They hunted rabbits and gathered wild plants they could use for food. They also developed a way to catch deer by digging pits along the river and hiding the pits with branches so the deer would fall into the trap.

The Central Tribes

South of the Modoc homeland, the climate was warmer and food more abundant. This huge region of central California was home to three-fifths of all Native Americans who lived in the state. Tribes in this area included the Miwok, Maidu, Yokut, Salinan, Costano, Esselen, and Pomo. People of these tribes hunted, fished, and gathered plants, such as nuts, berries, and herbs.

Acorns, which showered down from oak trees every fall, were one of the most important food sources to the central California tribes. People gathered the acorns and used stone tools to pound them into flour.

The Pomo tribe made its home in central California. A historic reconstruction of a Pomo dwelling is pictured here.

This acorn meal was later mixed with water and cooked into hot cereal which was eaten with honey, nuts, and berries, or with bits of meat.

Weaving Baskets

To store acorns for long periods of time, women made beautiful baskets from grasses, reeds, and roots. A woman might work for a year or more on a single basket if it was very large or very detailed. Tribe members wove baskets with their own special geometric designs, sometimes ornamented with feathers or shells. Basket fibers were colored red, yellow, and black with dyes made from berries, buttercups, sunflowers, onions, or indigo bushes.

Pomo women were believed to be the best basket makers in California. They made a great variety of well-designed baskets that were prized by all tribes and traded throughout the state.

The South Coast Tribes

The Pomo often traded with the Chumash tribe who lived in the southern California valleys and along the southern Pacific Coast. The Chumash built their shelters from reeds woven over willow frames. The dome-shaped shelters were covered with deerskins to keep out the rain.

The Chumash were great fishers and skilled boat-builders. Although they often fished with hooks, lines, nets, and basket traps, some were so skilled they were able to catch fish with their bare hands. The Chumash also feasted on shore birds, clams, shellfish, small game, and whales.

The Desert Tribes

The hot, dry desert of the Great Basin east of the Sierra Mountains was the least populated area of California. Tribes such as the Monachi, Owens Valley, and

Northern Paiute lived in small groups because food supplies were limited. The tribes often had to walk great distances in order to find food such as wild grass seeds and piñon nuts which grew on pine trees. They

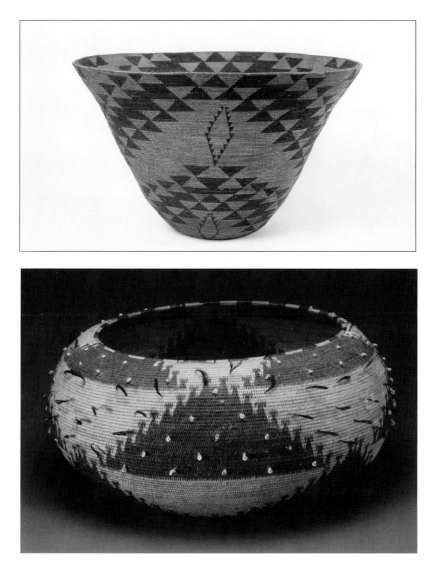

These beautiful baskets were crafted by members of the Maidu tribe (top) and the Pomo. Pomo women were thought to be the best basket makers in California.

also hunted rabbits, squirrels, and other small animals, and large game such as bighorn rams.

The possessions of the desert people were simple and lightweight. Individual families lived in sagebrush or rush huts, called wickiups. They used bows and

The desert tribes hunted small animals and also large game, such as this bighorn ram.

arrows to hunt and baskets for gathering and drying seeds. Blankets made from rabbit fur kept them warm during cool desert nights.

The people of the southwestern desert lived in tribes such as the Gabrielino, Luiseno, Cahuilla, and Diegueno. They ate the fruit of the fan palm, yucca, agave, and prickly pear cactus. Foods such as the berries of the manzanita, a shrub, the bulbs of the desert lily, and the beans of the mesquite bush also helped the tribes survive.

The desert people not only made soap from the root of the yucca tree but also baskets, sandals, and rope from the leaves of that plant. Wherever there was water in the desert, wild plums and apricots could also be found.

The Southeastern Tribes

Along the Colorado River in southeast California, tribes such as the Yuma and Mojave built earth shelters of mounded soil, which protected them from the hot desert sun. These Colorado River tribes were the only farmers in California and planted corn, beans, squash, and pumpkins. They also gathered wild foods such as the pods of the honey mesquite bush that were used to make a candylike treat. The blossoms of the honey mesquite were soaked for several days to make a thirst-quenching drink.

The southeastern tribes stored water, grains, and seeds in pottery jars they made from riverbed clay. These filled jars protected the food and drink from the hot desert sun and were left in cool caves for use in times of need.

Members of the Yuma tribe appear in this nineteenth-century portrait. The Yuma and the Mojave were the only farming tribes in California.

Harmony with Nature

California has always been a natural garden of berries, fruit, and food plants of great variety. The first people of California lived in harmony with nature, while depending on plants and wild animals for survival. The tribes rarely waged war on one another, choosing to live in peace while trading goods and sharing their knowledge of the land.

Chapter Two

Spanish Missions

The first known European to arrive in California was Juan Rodríguez Cabrillo, a Portuguese explorer employed by Spain. Cabrillo sailed into San Diego Bay in 1542. From there he sailed north along the coast, mapping the shoreline and visiting Native American tribes. Cabrillo visited Santa Catalina Island by Los Angeles, Point Reyes near San Francisco, and Monterey Bay.

The Portuguese explorer probably called the area California. By this time the west coast of Mexico had also been given that name, probably by Spanish explorer Hernán Cortes. Thinking that the land was an island, Cortes named the area after a fictional tropical island laden with gold mentioned in the Spanish romance novel *The Adventures of Esplandián*, by Garci Rodríguez de Montalvo (published around 1510).

When explorers learned that western Mexico was a finger of land attached to the mainland to the north,

An artist depicts the ship of Portuguese explorer Juan Rodríguez Cabrillo in colorful ceramic tile.

they called it Baja California (meaning Lower California, now part of Mexico). The northern region, which they called Alta California (Upper California), included present-day California.

More Explorers

The next European visitor to California was the English **navigator** Sir Francis Drake, who traveled to the area in 1579. Drake sailed up the coast as part of a three-year voyage around the world. The British explorer was under orders from English queen Elizabeth I to harass and raid Spanish settlements along the Pacific Coast. After filling his ship, the *Golden Hind,* with silver and gold plundered from Spanish towns in Baja California, the English navigator anchored his ship near present-day San Francisco to make repairs.

Drake stayed in Alta California for about five weeks. Members of the Miwok tribe gave his men fresh water

English navigator Sir Francis Drake sailed up the California coast in 1579, with orders from Queen Elizabeth I to raid Spanish settlements.

to drink, acorn bread, and dried berries. In return Drake gave them cloth, beads, and other trinkets. He named the land *Nova Albion,* Latin for "New England," and recommended the area as an ideal location for an English military base. Drake also claimed California for England, but the English did little to protect their claim in this land so distant from Europe.

Again, California remained unexplored by Europeans for many years. Then in 1602 Sebastián Vizcaíno explored the coast of Alta California for the king of Spain. He urged the king to let him found a colony at Monterey, but Spain was committed to **colonizing** Mexico first.

The First Mission

Spain did not begin to protect its interest in California until the 1760s, when Russian fur traders came to the area to hunt for seal and sea otter. Spain wanted to prevent Russia from claiming the area so the Spanish king sent Governor Gaspar de Portolá, Catholic missionary Father Junípero Serra, and a group of soldiers from Mexico to settle Alta California. They arrived in present-day San Diego in July 1769.

The Spanish set up a **presidio,** or military post, as well as a **mission.** The presidio was manned by soldiers and used as a trading post and supply house for military weapons. The mission was built in order to introduce Catholicism and European farming methods to the Native Americans in the region.

A statue of Father Junípero Serra stands on the beautiful grounds of the Mission of San Diego de Alcala, in present-day San Diego.

The Presidios

Between 1769 and 1782 the Spanish built three more missions and presidios in Santa Barbara, Monterey, and San Francisco. The presidios were needed to protect the missions from foreign invaders and Native American rebellion.

The presidios were surrounded with farm settlements known as **pueblos**. Cities such as San Jose and Los Angeles started out as small pueblos built around the forts. The pueblos were populated with poor Mexicans of mixed Spanish and Native American descent called **mestizos**. The mestizos worked the land and were forced to give most of their produce to government officials. The farmers were aided by Native American laborers that had been rounded up by Spanish soldiers.

Life at the Missions

Each mission on the coastal path known as El Camino Real, or the Royal Road, was built as a walled city with

The Mission of San Diego de Alcala, pictured here, was built by the Spanish to introduce Catholicism and farming to native tribes.

El Presidio, in Santa Barbara, was one of several military posts built by the Spanish to protect California missions.

two entrances. Heavy wood and metal gates were closed at night to keep attackers out and the laborers inside.

The climate in California is very much like that of Spain, so Spanish crops thrived there. The slaves tended olive trees and grapevines that had been brought from Spain, as well as herds of Spanish cattle.

The Native Americans worked as bakers, blacksmiths, candle makers, carpenters, cooks, farmers, irrigation ditchdiggers, masons, potters, shepherds, tile makers, weavers, wine makers, and woodworkers, among other trades. Much of what they produced was sent to the Spanish government in Mexico in the form of wine, olive oil, leather, food, and other goods.

Hard Life for Native Americans

The Native Americans faced great difficulties. Families were split up and everyone had to work from dawn until dusk, even the children. They were housed in crowded, dirty huts, and many died of European diseases such as smallpox. Uprooted, enslaved, and stripped of their identity, few Native Americans were able to survive more than ten years under the mission system.

Some laborers managed to escape. Those who were caught and returned to the missions were cruelly punished. Others got away but carried European diseases with them, which spread to tribes all over the state, killing thousands.

In 1775, two runaways, Francisco and Zegota, escaped from presidio soldiers and organized a rebellion, burning down the mission at San Diego. Hostile warriors made

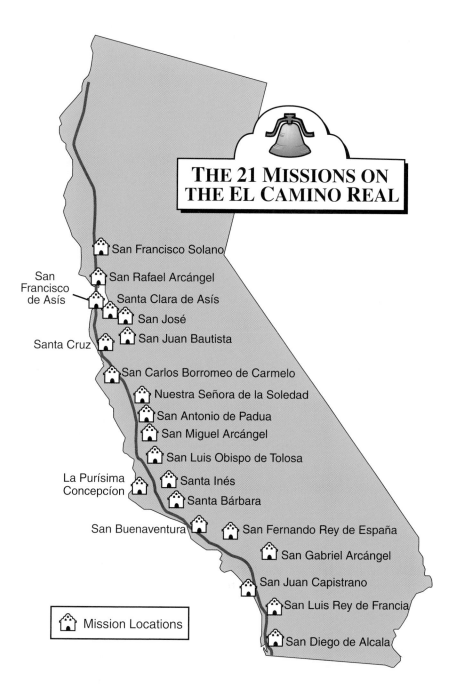

THE 21 MISSIONS ON THE EL CAMINO REAL

San Francisco Solano

San Rafael Arcángel

San Francisco de Asís

Santa Clara de Asís

San José

San Juan Bautista

Santa Cruz

San Carlos Borromeo de Carmelo

Nuestra Señora de la Soledad

San Antonio de Padua

San Miguel Arcángel

San Luis Obispo de Tolosa

La Purísima Concepcíon

Santa Inés

Santa Bárbara

San Buenaventura

San Fernando Rey de España

San Gabriel Arcángel

San Juan Capistrano

San Luis Rey de Francia

San Diego de Alcala

Mission Locations

Native Americans worked long hours at the missions. Those pictured here are making baskets and rope.

overland roads dangerous and discouraged Spanish settlers from coming in from Mexico. As a result, the Spanish maintained their power along the coast, but could not move inland to conquer the rest of the state.

The Booming Fur Trade

From their coastal presidios, the Spanish tried to keep hunters, settlers, and traders out of their colony. They passed laws to ban sailors from other countries from coming ashore to hunt or trade. But seals and otters were abundant along the coast, and traders came from many countries seeking their rich, thick furs.

British, French, and U.S. ships came to trade with coastal settlements, breaking Spanish law. Russian fur traders, who had bases in present-day Alaska, increased their hunting along California's coast. In spite of Spanish protest, they bought a large parcel of land near San Francisco. They bought the land from the Kayasha tribe in exchange for three blankets, three pairs of trousers, two axes, three hoes, and some beads.

In 1812, Russian fur traders built an outpost called Fort Ross on this land. They trapped seals and sea otters and shipped their furs to China, trading for rich goods from the Orient. Other traders followed this pattern, until the sea otter became almost extinct.

A modern-day otter floats peacefully along the California coast. These creatures were much prized by eighteenth-century hunters and fur traders for their excellent fur.

Fort Ross, pictured here, was built by Russian fur traders.

Still, more people came to California. The climate was warm, the land fertile, and the oil, timber, and minerals were abundant. In the early years of the nineteenth century, farmers, hunters, and traders from countries across the globe flooded into the area, and Spain began to lose control of its rich and distant colony.

Chapter Three

The Mexican Ranchos

In 1821, people in Mexico revolted against Spanish rule and soon won their freedom. The next year, the Spanish **empire** in the New World was further weakened when Mexico claimed all land in Alta California.

The central Mexican government far away in Mexico City was torn by revolution, however. The office of governor changed hands dozens of times, often because of uprisings and revolutions rather than elections.

During the era of Mexican rule, which lasted into the 1840s, the Mexican government shipped convicts and political prisoners north to Alta California. These men started revolutions and committed crimes. But the biggest revolutionary change came when the mission system was brought to an end.

In 1833, the Mexican Congress ordered the closing of all missions, including the Mission of San Carlos Borromeo de Carmelo, pictured here as it looks today.

The End of the Missions

In 1833, the Mexican Congress ordered the missions to be closed and the mission lands to be divided among the Native Americans who worked as mission slaves. Confusion and land grabbing followed this government order as Spanish cattle ranchers seized most of the mission lands, leaving only the worst land for the tribes.

By 1846, 8 million acres of mission land were broken up into eight hundred huge privately owned cattle ranches, called **ranchos**. Most of the land was taken by several hundred powerful men, including army veterans, and friends and relatives of the Mexican governors. The governors also gave away the stock owned by the missions that included 370,000 cattle, 62,000 horses, and 320,000 sheep, hogs, and goats. Unused mission buildings were turned into hotels, bars, stores, warehouses, restaurants, workshops, and houses.

Enticed by the government giveaway, thousands of people from Mexico came to the area and made false claims on lands left to the Native Americans. The former slaves on these lands were ordered to move, and no one was powerful enough to defend their legal claims.

Spanish cattle ranchers seized most of the mission lands, turning them into ranchos like the one pictured here.

Nowhere to Go

Many of the Native Americans tried to go back to their old ways of life, but they had nowhere to live. Some walked out to the desert, where they suffered from hunger. Many went to work in the growing towns of Los Angeles, San Diego, Santa Barbara, and San Jose. In Los Angeles, Native American workers labored under slavelike conditions and were paid only in liquor. Others had little choice but to work on the giant ranchos in exchange for food, clothing, and shelter.

When the Mexican Congress closed the missions, many Native American mission slaves looked for work in towns such as Los Angeles, pictured here as it looked in 1855.

Since Native Americans did most of the work on the ranchos, the rancho owners had plenty of leisure time and frequently held festive gatherings, some lasting for more than a week.

Native American men worked in construction, labored in the fields, gathered and cut timber, and raised cattle and sheep on the ranchos. Women worked as servants, maids, cooks, and nannies.

The Good Life

Because most of the work was done by Native Americans, rancheros had a lot of free time to entertain guests and enjoy life. Social life on the ranchos was a lively round of feasts, festivals, weddings, christenings, wakes, cockfights, and horseback races. Church holidays such as All Saints Day also provided reason for celebration.

L. E. SMOOT MEMORIAL LIBRARY
299533 KINGS HIGHWAY
KING GEORGE, VA 22485

Parties sometimes lasted a week or more. Guests were served large portions of food and drink. Women dressed in bright velvets and men in embroidered jackets. They played violins, guitars, cymbals, and drums, and danced the night away.

The Rodeo

The most exciting social gatherings happened twice a year during roundup time. Because the ranchos had no fences, huge herds of semiwild cattle grazed together on shared land. In spring, the cattle had to be rounded up, separated, and counted. Marks that showed who owned the animals were branded onto the sides of the cattle with a hot iron. Every ranchero had a different symbol or letters for their brand and each was registered in a special book.

When the roundup work was over, it was time for the rodeos to begin. People traveled from all over to see these rodeos, and they were the biggest social events of the year. Cattle were killed and barbecued in pits dug into the earth. Large shelters were built from brush and reeds for music, drinking, and dancing.

The rodeo could last a week or more and included contests with cattle roping and bronco riding. The rancheros bet on horse races and other games. In one such game, a live chicken was buried in the ground up to its neck. Horsemen rode by at a full gallop and tried to pull the chicken out of the hole.

Huge herds of cattle were branded during the spring roundup.

California Bank Notes

The spring roundup was repeated in the fall. Herds of cattle were rounded up and herded to the coast to be slaughtered. Cattle needed to be taken to the coast and sold because that was where people purchased the cattle for food.

During the fall, cattle were rounded up to be slaughtered and sold.

Cow fat, called tallow, was important for use in candles and soap. Bulls' horns were used to make buttons, knife handles, and other products. Cowhides were so valued for leather, that they were used as money and came to be known as California bank notes.

During the fall roundup, ships came from all over the world to trade for the cattle. In exchange, they traded goods such as farm tools, shoes, cotton clothing, and tea and silks from China. Sometimes the ships stayed weeks, or even months.

The sailors who came to trade in California were welcomed into the homes of the cattle ranchers. After the sailors left, they spread the word about California, a place where life seemed happy and carefree. People started to come from many places to enjoy the good life in Alta California, and the population of the state began to grow.

Chapter Four

The Bear Flag Republic

The riches of California beckoned to many, and Americans who wanted free land in California only needed to accept Mexican citizenship and practice the Catholic religion.

The first Americans who went to California were mainly explorers, traders, and sailors who arrived in ships. In 1827, the first fur trapper who walked to California from the East was Jedediah Smith. Leading a ragged band of beaver trappers, Smith blazed a trail across the Mojave desert and over the Sierra Nevada mountain range. When he returned to the East, he published a story of his journey in a magazine, and encouraged adventurers to hike overland to California.

Many settlers followed Smith's advice, including John Sutter, a German immigrant who arrived in California in 1834. Five years later, the Mexican governor

Modern horsemen of the American Mountain Men Association retrace the route of famed fur trapper Jedediah Smith.

of California granted Sutter a large parcel of land in the Sacramento Valley.

To add to his holdings, Sutter bought Fort Ross, the old Russian fur trading post. This huge estate became known as Sutter's Fort, and it provided shelter for many American settlers arriving in California. By 1840, several hundred settlers from the United States had joined the several thousand Hispanic settlers who previously lived in Alta California.

Before long, groups of midwesterners began to organize overland trips to California. In 1841, John Bidwell and John Bartleson led the first wagon train to

California. It was a long, hard trip across plains, deserts, and mountains. The travelers often faced bad weather, and many died from disease or hunger.

Manifest Destiny

Most of the new Californians settled in the fertile valleys of Sacramento and San Joachín. They were average farmers or shopkeepers but a few became wealthy merchants or powerful government officials. Many of these settlers wanted California to become part of the United States. President James Knox Polk also wanted the United States to include California.

This nineteenth-century painting depicts the city of Sacramento. Many new settlers made their homes in the Sacramento valley.

Joyful men raise a homemade bear flag, declaring California's independence from Mexico.

In 1845, Polk tried to buy California and other parts of the Southwest from Mexico, but Mexican officials refused the offer. These events soon led to war between Mexico and the United States.

The Mexican-American War

On June 14, 1846, U.S. settlers captured the presidio at Sonoma, north of San Francisco. They proclaimed their freedom from Mexican rule and renamed Alta California the California Republic. The uprising was called the Bear Flag Revolt because the rebels raised a homemade flag with a picture of a grizzly bear, a star, a red stripe, and the words *California Republic* on it.

The flag is still California's state flag, but the republic lasted only twenty-three days. On July 7, 1846, Commodore John D. Sloat, commander of the U.S. naval forces along the California coast, ordered the U.S. flag raised at Monterey and claimed California for the United States.

In August, Sloat's replacement, Commodore Robert F. Stockton, set up a U.S. territorial government in California and named himself governor. In September, Mexican soldiers led by Captain José Maria Flores attacked the new republic and regained control over much of California south of San Luis Obispo.

A few months later, in December 1846, a U.S. force of about one hundred men commanded by General Stephen W. Kearny arrived in California. While trying to take San Pasqual, near present-day Escondido, Kearny's men were defeated by Mexican soldiers and forced to retreat.

On January 10, 1847, Kearny's soldiers joined forces with Stockton's troops to capture Los Angeles. After this defeat, Mexico agreed to accept the rule of the United States. On February 2, 1848, they signed the Treaty of Guadalupe Hidalgo, ending the Mexican-American War. Mexico gave up a large portion of territory to the United States, including present-day New Mexico, Arizona, and California.

The Gold Rush

On January 24, just nine days before the Treaty of Guadalupe Hidalgo was signed, a carpenter named

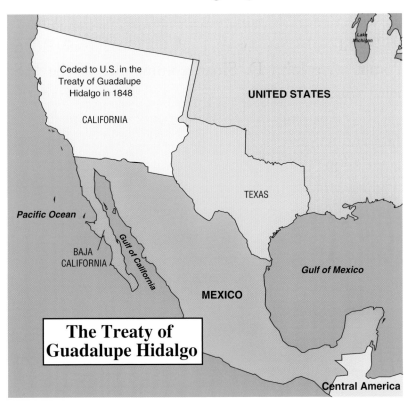

James Wilson Marshall was building a grain mill for John Sutter when he found gold in the American River. News of his discovery soon traveled to San Francisco, and almost every man in town rushed off to look for gold.

Gold fever quickly swept through the towns along the coast. By fall the news had spread all over the United States, Mexico, South America, and even to Europe. Within months, people were coming from all over the world to strike it rich in California, which by now was a U.S. territory.

Gold prospectors came by wagon, stagecoach, and boat; on horseback and on foot. Thousands of ships came from Mexico, South America, Hawaii, Europe,

Australia, and China. When the ships arrived, the captains and sailors often ran off with everyone else in search for gold. San Francisco harbor was cluttered with abandoned ships.

In 1849 alone, about seventy-five thousand miners, called forty-niners, came to California, swelling the population of the state to ninety thousand. Few women joined the forty-niners, since crime was rampant and living conditions were very harsh.

Life in the Mining Camps

The wild hills of northern California were suddenly covered with the canvas tents of mining camps with colorful names like Hell's Delight and Poker Flats. No camp was complete without a gambling saloon, where drunken brawls were often settled with knives and pistols.

Because food and other supplies had to be brought in over long distances to reach the camps, life was very expensive in mining towns. Many people opened businesses to serve the needs of the miners and made huge profits selling shovels, tools, cookware, and clothing. Blue-jean maker Levi Strauss began a clothing empire by selling tough denim pants to miners.

The sudden swarm of rough and lawless gold seekers led to further destruction of the Native American tribes, however. They once again faced epidemics of smallpox and other diseases. Many starved when they were pushed off their land. Some gold-seekers were so hungry for land, they shot any Native American they saw. Some Native Americans managed to escape to the mountains or the deserts.

Becoming a State

Miners trespassed on the property of Native Americans, Mexicans, and Americans alike. They dug channels, redirected streams, cut down trees, and removed rocks to get to the gold. John Sutter was forced into bankruptcy. His land claim was destroyed by miners, and he became bitter, claiming all the gold in California belonged to him.

The gold rush attracted thousands of men hoping to make their fortunes in California.

California was in a state of complete confusion as American law, Mexican law, and military law mingled with crime, greed, and destruction.

With so many people arriving daily, California badly needed strict laws and government supervision. On June 3, 1849, the military governor, General Bennet Riley, called for a convention to draw up a **constitution** for California. California's new constitution was modeled on that of Iowa, which had just become a state. The convention formalized the boundaries of California and declared the territory a state.

The convention elected state officials, a **legislature,** and two senators, who were sent to Washington. Although California was acting as a state, only Congress

The proud flag of California carries the emblem of the grizzly bear to this day.

was allowed to create a new state. So California's two senators, John C. Frémont and William M. Gwin, were not allowed to take their seats. After months of argument, Congress finally allowed California to become a state. President Millard Fillmore signed the California statehood bill on September 9, 1850, and California became the thirty-first state. California, named after a mythical land laden with gold, has proved itself to be a land of golden opportunity.

Facts About California

State capital: Sacramento

Largest city: Los Angeles

State motto: *Eureka* (I have found it)

State song: "I Love You, California"

State nickname: Golden State

State flower: golden poppy

State insect: California dog-face butterfly

State tree: California redwood

State animal: California grizzly bear

State marine mammal: California gray whale

State bird: California valley quail

State fish: South Fork golden trout

State rock: serpentine

State fossil: saber-toothed tiger

State mineral: gold

Famous people: Ansel Adams, Shirley Temple Black, Jerry Brown, Joe DiMaggio, Clint Eastwood, Dianne Feinstein, Robert Frost, William Randolph Hearst, Jack London, Marilyn Monroe, Richard Nixon, John Steinbeck, Adlai Stevenson, Earl Warren

Glossary

colonize: To create a settlement governed by a distant country.

constitution: The basic laws of a government.

empire: A number of nations ruled by a single political authority.

legislature: A group of people who make laws for a nation or state.

mestizo: A person of mixed Native American and Spanish ancestry.

mission: A group of buildings housing people sent by a religious organization to establish relations in a foreign land.

navigator: A person who plans and controls the movement of a ship.

presidio: A fort established by the Spanish to protect their missions.

pueblo: Adobe apartment rooms built around a central plaza.

rancho: A huge privately owned cattle ranch.

For Further Exploration

Books

Sonia Bleeker, *The Mission Indians of California*. New York: William Morrow, 1956. A moving personal story combined with an authentic description of the way of life centered around the Spanish missions of California.

Gail Faber and Michele Lasagna, *Whispers from the First Californians*. Alamo, CA: Magpie Publications, 1980. This book provides factual information as well as giving readers a deeper understanding and appreciation for the first people of California.

Ann Heinrichs, *California*. New York: Childrens Press, 1998. A brief introduction to the geography, history, natural resources, industries, cities, and people of California.

C. L. Keyworth, *California Indians*. New York: Facts On File, 1991. Examines the history, culture, changing fortunes, and current situation of the various Native American peoples of California.

Charles A. Wills, *A Historical Album of California*. Brookfield, CT: Millbrook Press, 1994. A history of California, from its early exploration and settlement to the state today with its unique status and influence on America.

Websites

The California Historical Society website. An illustrated guide to more than 300 years of California history, starting with the native cultures of the first Californians. www.calhist.org.

The official California State site includes a section called History and Culture of California. Includes maps, links to other California history sites, and essays about historical events and peoples. www.ca.gov.

Index

California

L.E. SMOOT MEMORIAL LIBRARY

3 1150 1002 9427 7

J   Boekhoff, P. M.
979.4   (Patti Marlene),
Boe   California

L. E. SMOOT MEMORIAL LIBRARY
9533 KINGS HIGHWAY
KING GEORGE, VA 22485

L. E. SMOOT MEMORIAL LIBRARY
9533 KINGS HIGHWAY
KING GEORGE, VA 22485